SIMPLE PRINTING METHODS

Materials	5
How to Start	6
Printing with Textures	12
Printing from Natural Objects	20
String Prints	28
Pencil and Crayon Rubbings	31
Potato and Cork Prints	38
Printing from Linoleum	40
String and Felt Collage Blocks	44

Simple Printing Methods

Jeanne Cross

S.G. Phillips, Inc.
New York

Copyright © 1972 by Jeanne Cross

All Rights Reserved. No part of this publication may be reproduced, stored in a retrieval system, or transmitted, in any form or by any means, electronic, mechanical, photocopying, recording or otherwise, without the prior permission of S. G. Phillips, Inc.

Library of Congress Catalog Card Number: 72-39812

JUV
NE
860
.C76

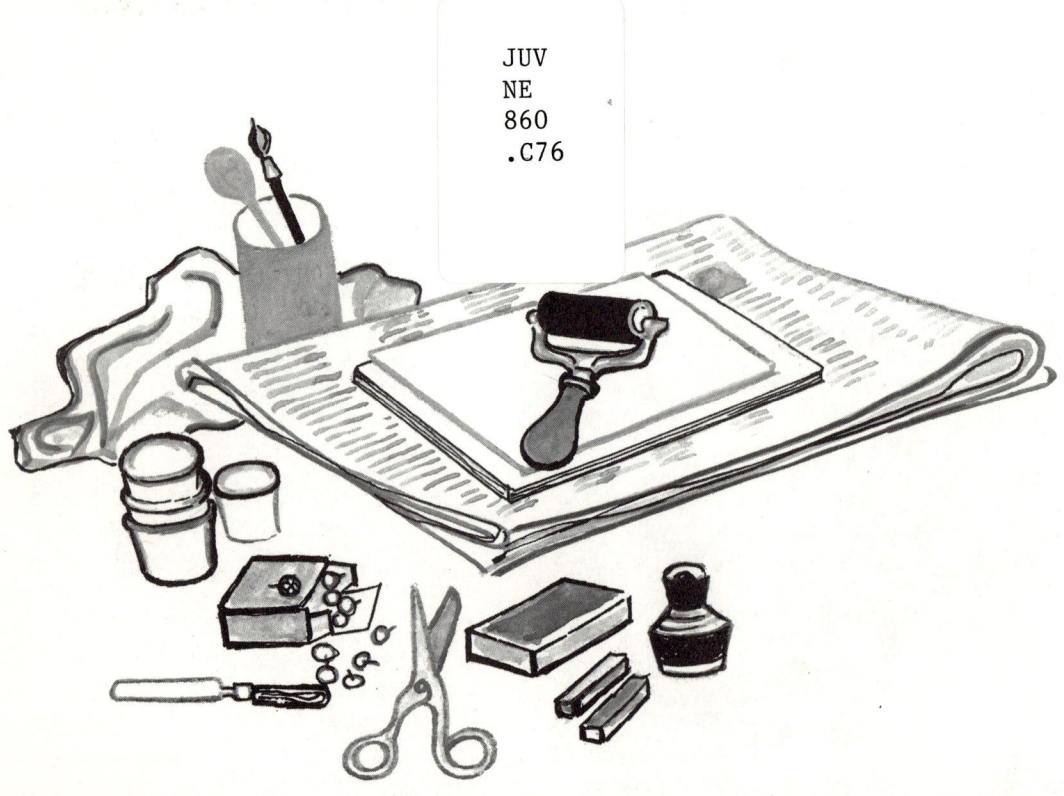

ISBN: 87599-192-0
Printed in England by Ebenezer Baylis & Son Ltd, Leicester and bound by William Brendon, Tiptree

SIMPLE PRINTING METHODS

This is a book about different methods of making prints on paper, with ink or crayon. The materials are all easy to obtain and easy to use.

Before you start you will need the following:
   A lino printing roller (obtainable at an art shop);
   A sheet of window glass, slightly smaller than your paper, and not too thin because it must not crack; glass with bevelled edges would be safest;
   Tubes of water-colour printing ink (oil inks cannot be washed away with water; they are also very slow-drying, and so unsuitable for flimsy paper);
   Some flimsy typing paper; a large amount of newspapers and cardboard; a kitchen knife; a tablespoon; coloured ink; a very soft pencil; wax crayons; drawing-pins; and blackboard chalk.
   Heavy paper clips are useful as you can string them along a line to hang up your prints to dry.

One or two other materials are mentioned in the text, but the list above is basic.

How to Start

Cover the table with newspapers and keep the supply of clean paper well away from the glass and the ink. Lay the glass flat on a pad of newspaper, and squeeze out a small blob of ink onto it.

Then take the roller and roll the ink out until it makes a thin, even coat. This is called 'rolling up'. Don't go over the edges of the glass!

Now run the roller over a clean piece of paper in different directions — and you will have your first print.

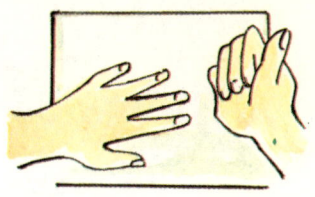

You can add blobs of another colour to the glass and roll these up as well; try experimenting with this, and see how the colours mix together.

Another way to print is to place a piece of paper directly onto the inky glass. When you have laid the paper in position, press down firmly with your fist all over it. Then lift up one corner to see if the ink has taken evenly; if so, peel off the paper gently from one side.

So far you have only been able to vary the design by using different colours, and by the way you use the roller; so here are some simple ways to make designs.

Roll up the ink again until you have an even surface, and try blocking out some of the background with torn strips of paper. Press the paper shapes into the inked surface, making sure that they are not being creased.

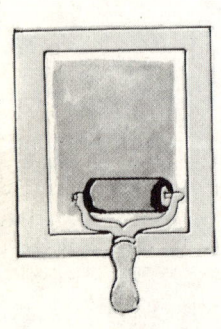  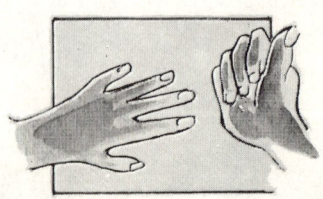

Then place a piece of paper over your design on the glass, and press firmly down with your fist again to make a print. As you lift off the paper all your shapes will appear in white.

The little circles left by a paper punch could be useful, or paper shapes made by folding and cutting.

Now try drawing designs in the ink. If you place the glass on a sheet of white paper, your design will show through more clearly. Clean the glass under the tap, dry it, and roll up the ink again until you have a thin, even patch; then, with the wooden end of a paintbrush, draw a design through the ink.

When you have finished, carefully place a sheet of paper so that it completely covers your design, and take a print as before.

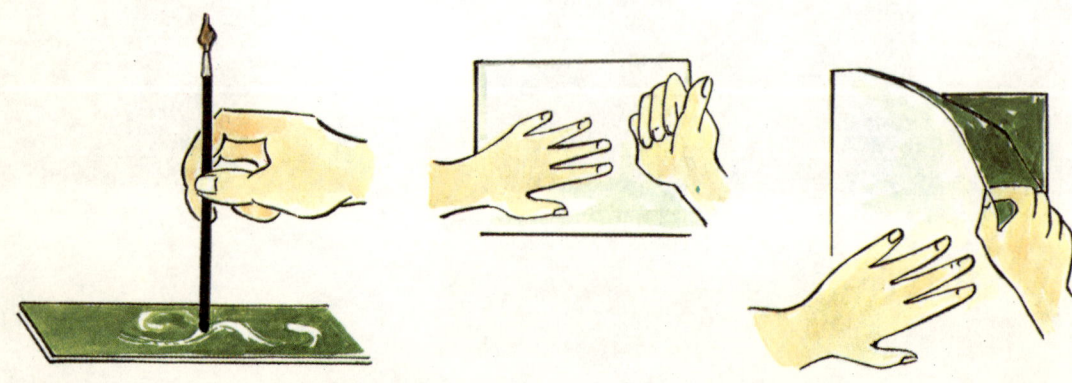

The design below was made using both methods I have described.

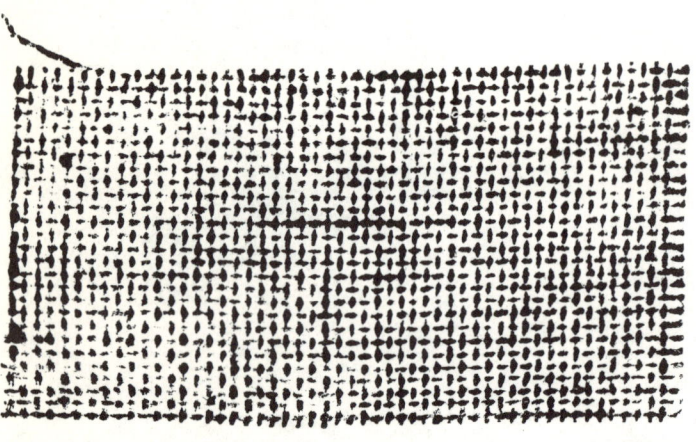

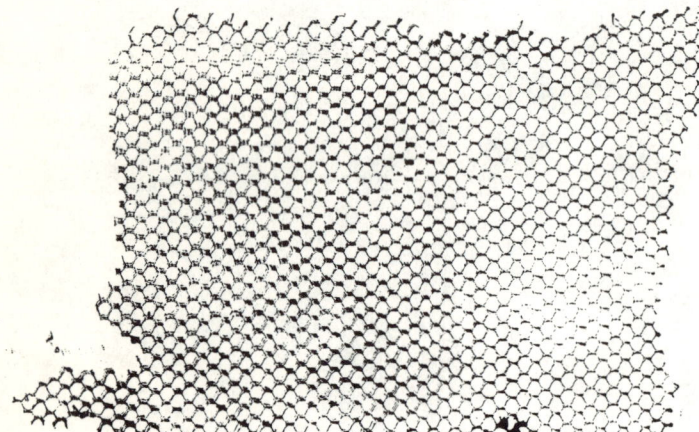

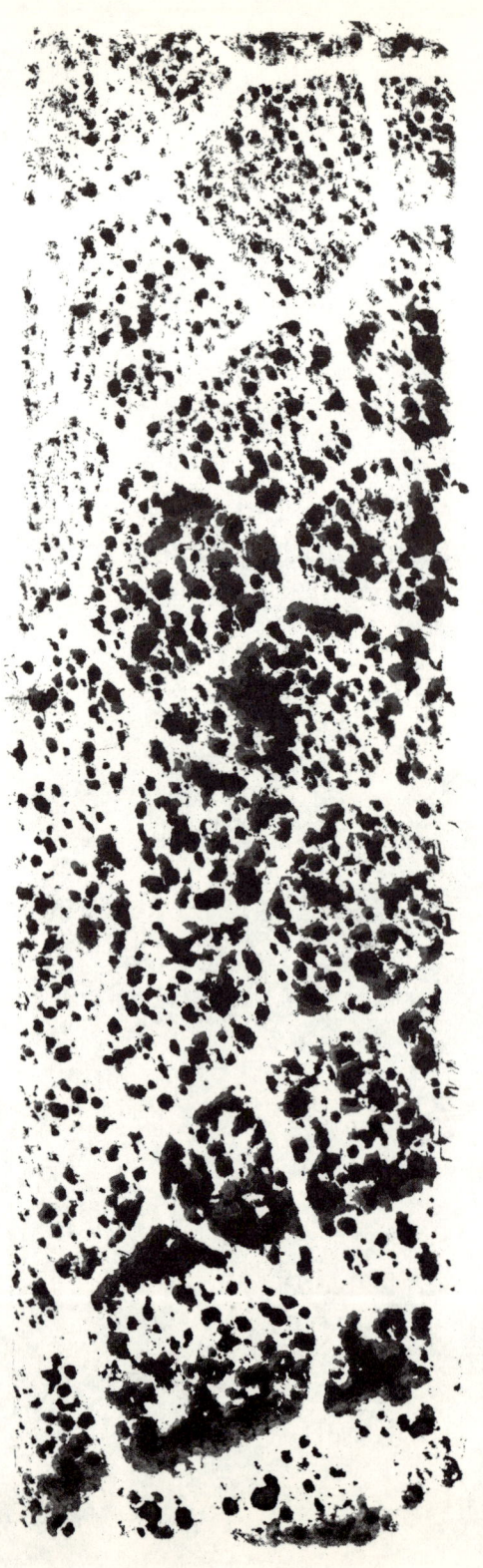

Printing with Textures
Here is a different way of printing. First make a collection of some interesting textured fabrics and materials; the illustrations show hessian, netting, frosted glass and wood.

Put whatever you want to print on a pad of newspaper. Squeeze out a blob of ink on the glass, and roll it up until the roller has a good coat of ink. If this is too sticky, add single drops of water to thin it down. Then roll the inky roller over the object you want to print.

To print from solid material like frosted glass or wood, lay a piece of paper over the inky surface and press down on top with your fist. Be careful not to smudge the print as you peel off the paper.

For flimsy material, like net or string, you should lift it from the newspaper onto a clean piece of paper and lay another piece on top. Then press down with your fist as before. This way you make two prints, one on the top and one on the bottom.

The print will be clearer if you use the back of a tablespoon to smooth down the top paper. This is called 'burnishing'.

For this one, contact glue was squeezed onto a triangular piece of wood and allowed to dry.

The patterns of glue on the surface were then inked and printed in the way described on page 14.

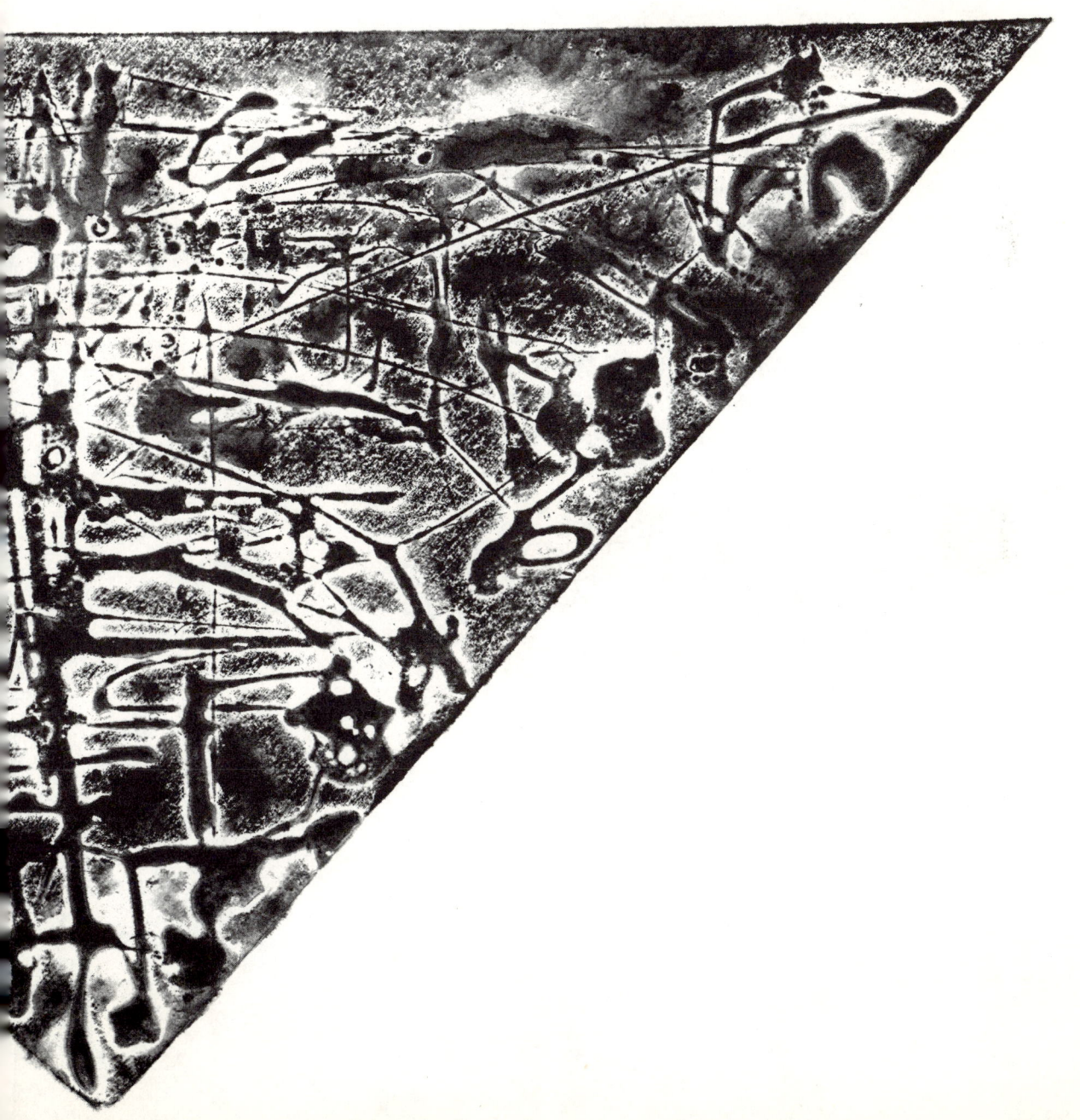

Corrugated paper can be cut into strips, circles or squares. Put the pieces onto newspaper and roll them up with ink; then press them onto another sheet of paper.

Simple designs can easily be built up by using the same piece of corrugated paper and making repeated patterns.

Printing from Natural Objects

Perhaps you live by the sea, and already have a collection of seagulls' feathers, seaweed, driftwood, stones and shells. These are printed in just the same way as textured surfaces.

Roll them up with ink as before, and then transfer them onto a clean sheet of paper and print carefully. The easiest way to do it is given on page 14.

This is a combination print. First the stones were inked separately and pressed into the middle, and then the blue was put on with the roller (see page 6).

These prints were made by placing the feathers on a clean sheet of paper and rolling the ink over them; when they were lifted off, their shape appeared in white. This is called 'printing in reverse'.

 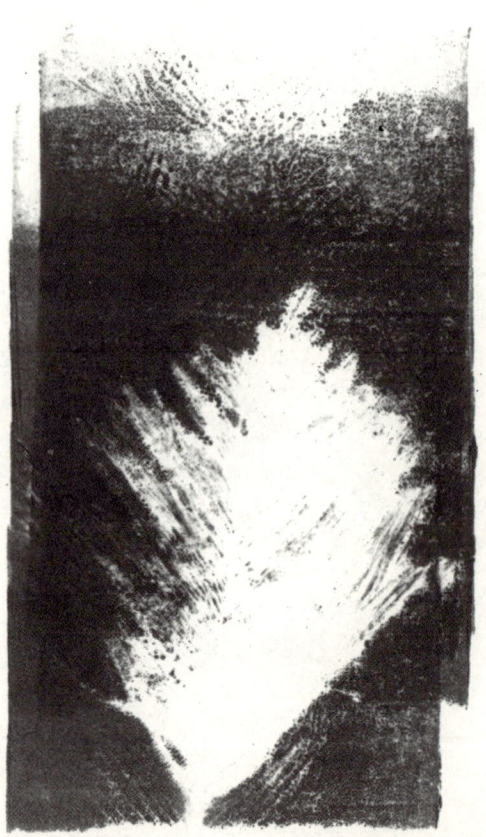

If you live in the country, you can make a collection of leaves, plants and mosses to print from. Print these like the flimsy material (page 14).

String Prints

First chalk a piece of paper with a stick of chalk. Hold the chalk flat to the paper, and make a few sweeping strokes over the surface.

Then dip a length of string into some ink, and let it drip onto some newspaper until it is just damp. Arrange the string onto the chalked paper, leaving one end hanging off the side; place another sheet of paper on top, and press down with one hand.

Now pull the string completely out from under the paper, still pressing down with your other hand. Carefully lift off the top sheet, and you will have a string print.

Try experimenting with shapes and colours; you can use coloured paper as well.

Pencil and Crayon Rubbings

Have you ever made a print of a penny with pencil and paper? If you put the penny under the paper, and rub the pencil over the top, the design comes through clearly.

All you need is more flimsy paper, a very soft pencil and a wax crayon. This is easier than a pencil for the larger prints, because it covers more space and will not tear the paper.

Coins, textured glass, wood and woven materials make excellent surfaces. Rub over the area with a wax crayon, taking care not to go over the outer edges of the image under the paper.

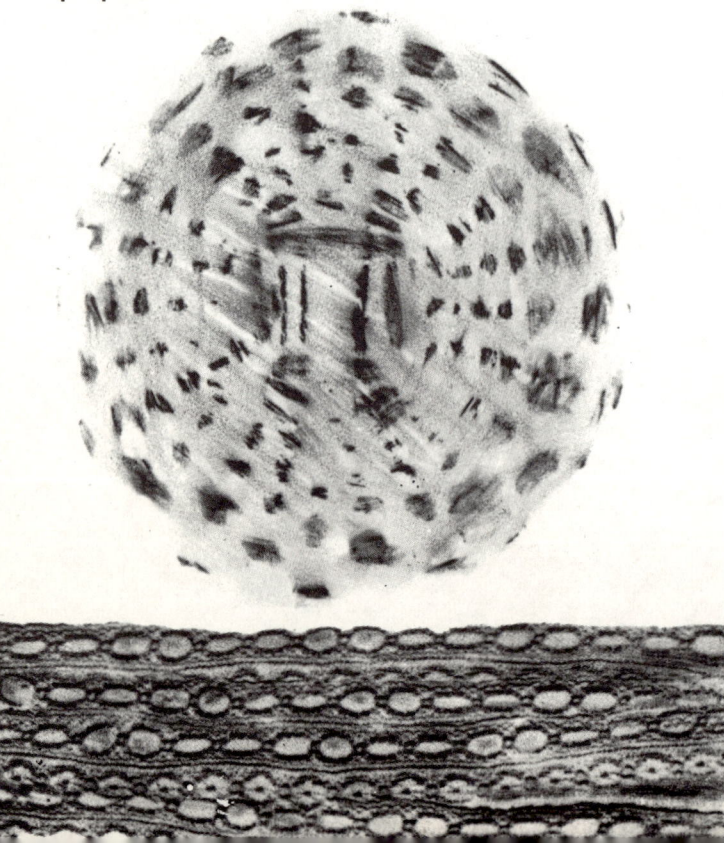

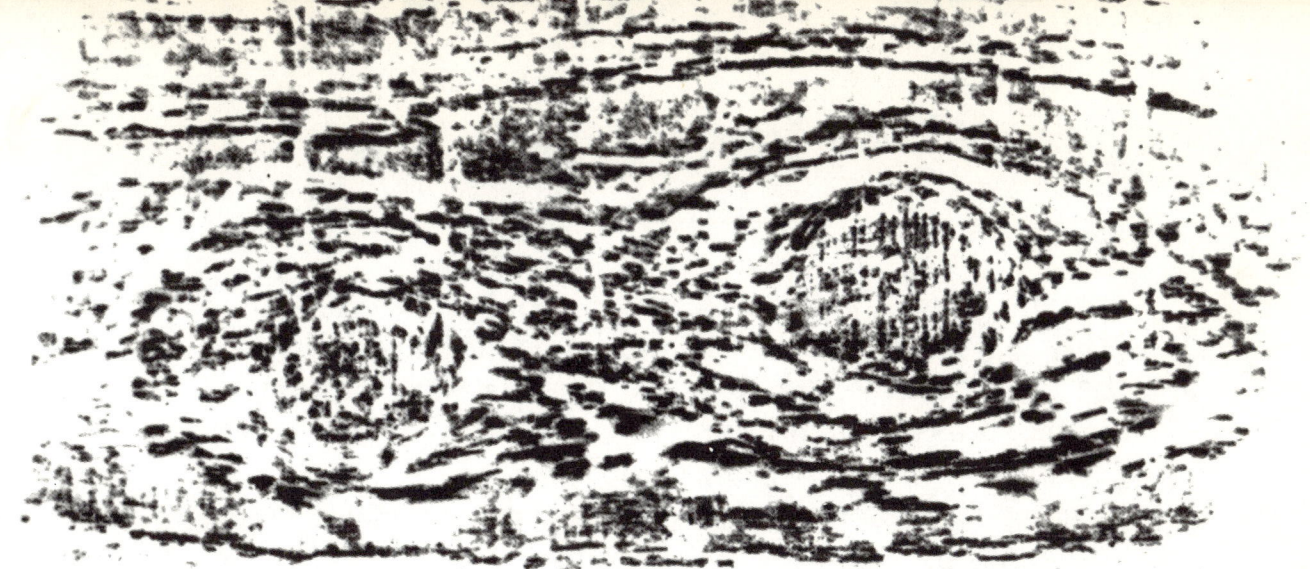

You can make a print by rubbing a dark crayon over light paper, or a light-coloured crayon over dark paper.

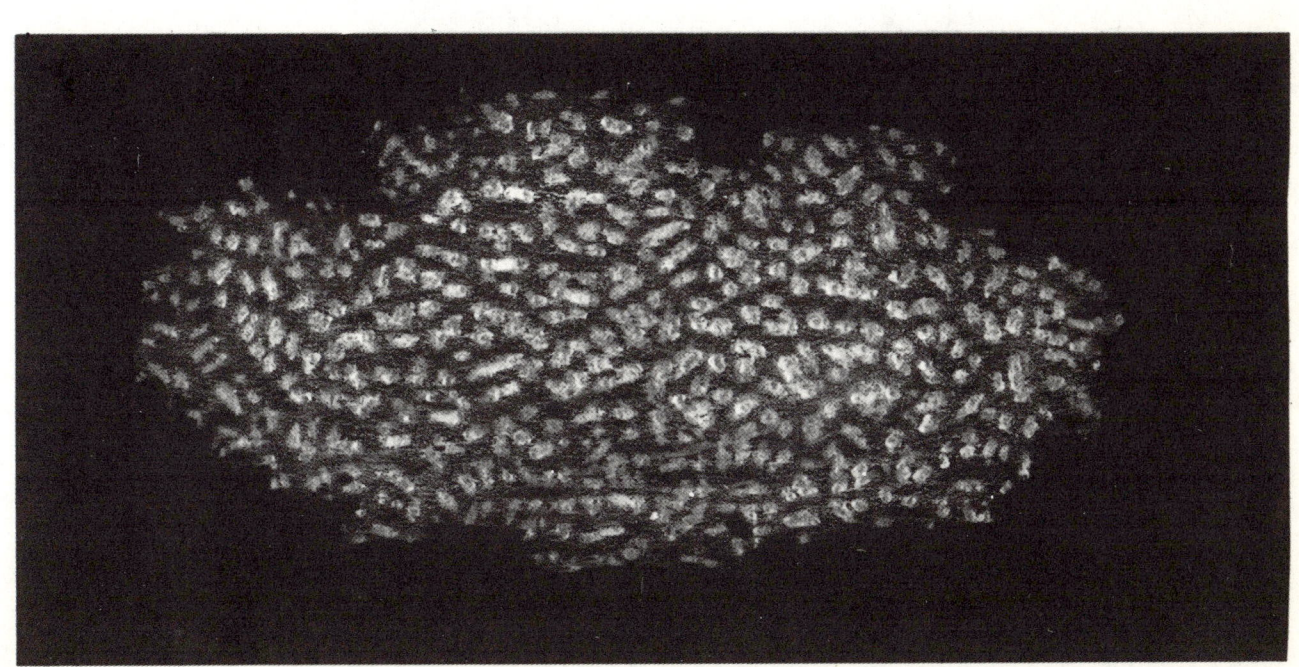

For the larger prints, like brass rubbings, you need a fairly large roll of paper. White lining or ceiling paper is the most suitable, and you can get this from decorators' shops. Brass rubbings are made with heelball, which consists of tallow, beeswax and lamp-black, and is sold by some shoe repair shops. You must get permission from someone in authority in the church before making rubbings in a church or cathedral.

 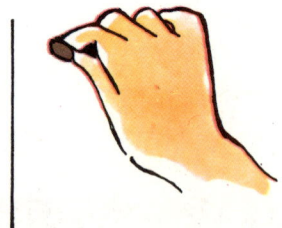

First carefully brush away any dirt, dust or grit from the surface as these can damage the print. Then roll out the paper and secure the top edges with weights or books. When the paper is lined up over the image, rub the heelball evenly over the whole area you want to print, taking care not to go over the outer edges.

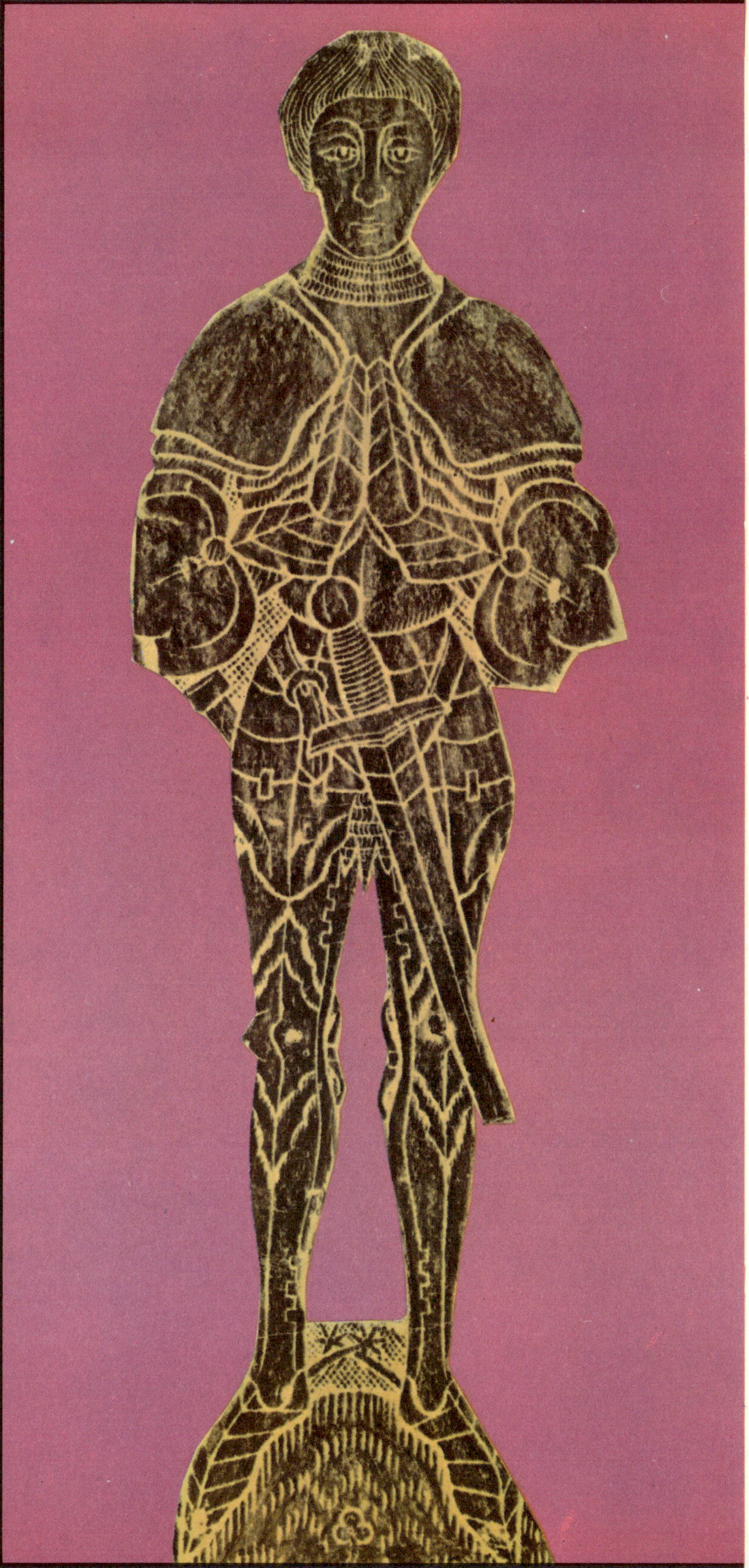

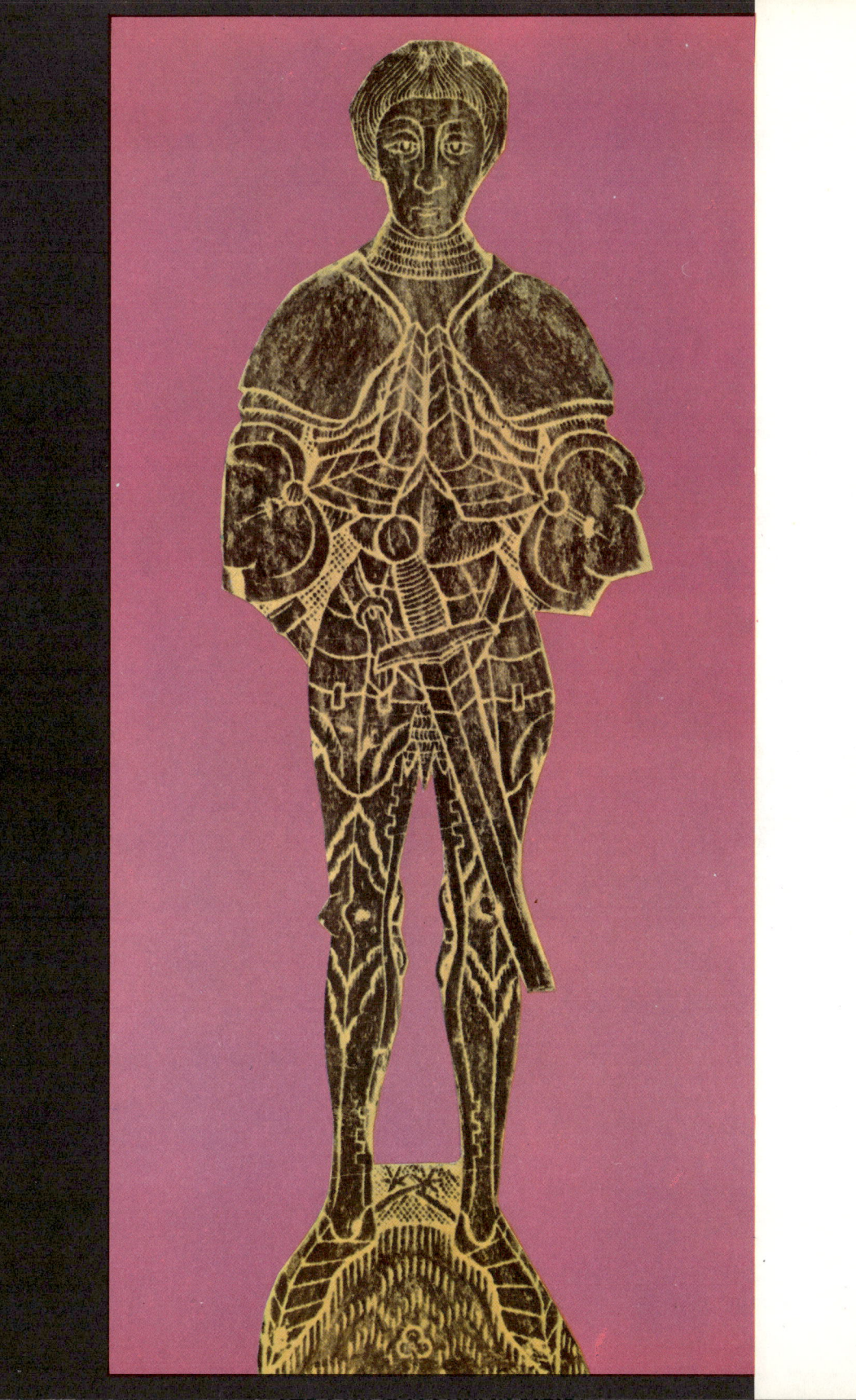

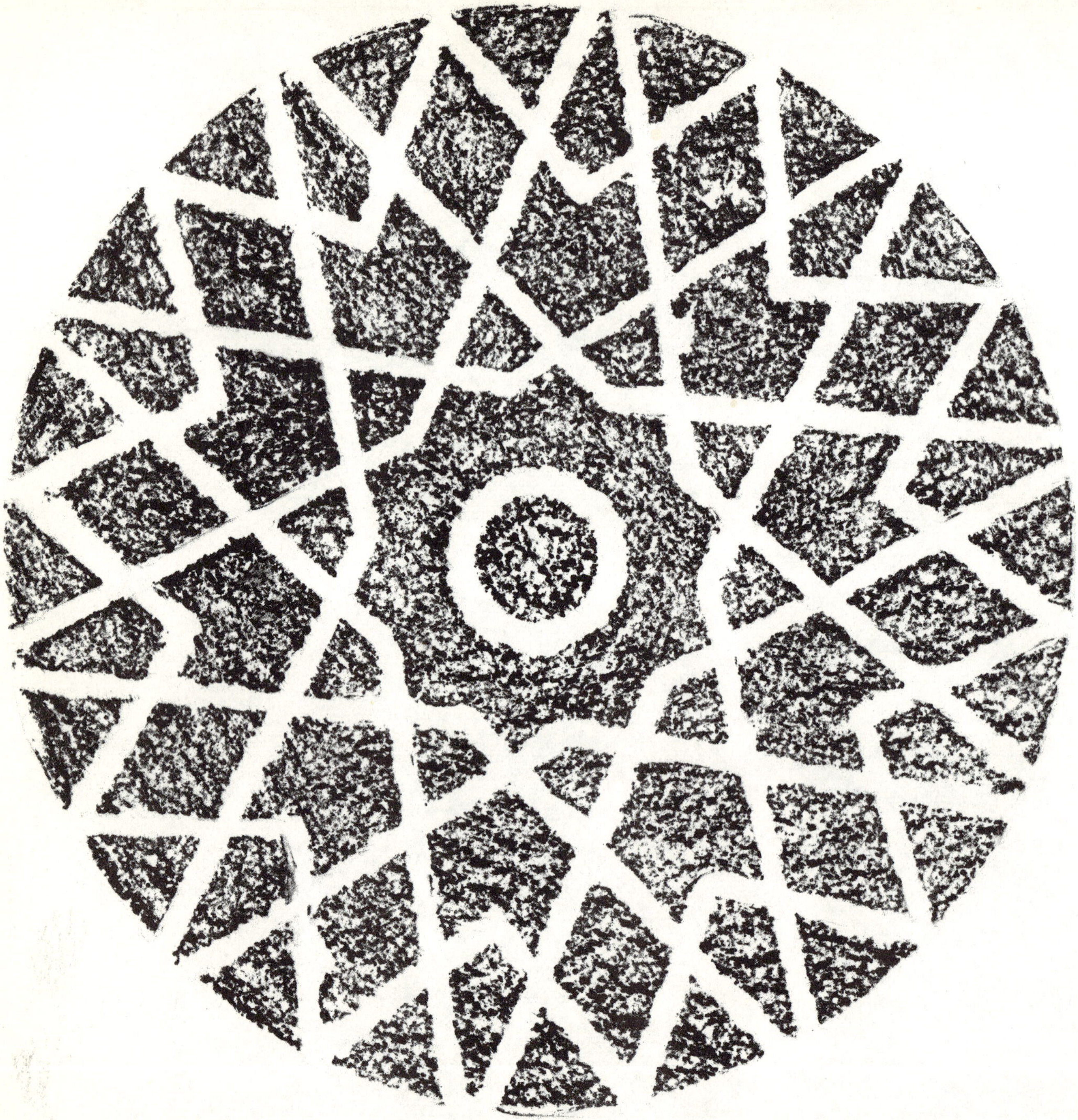

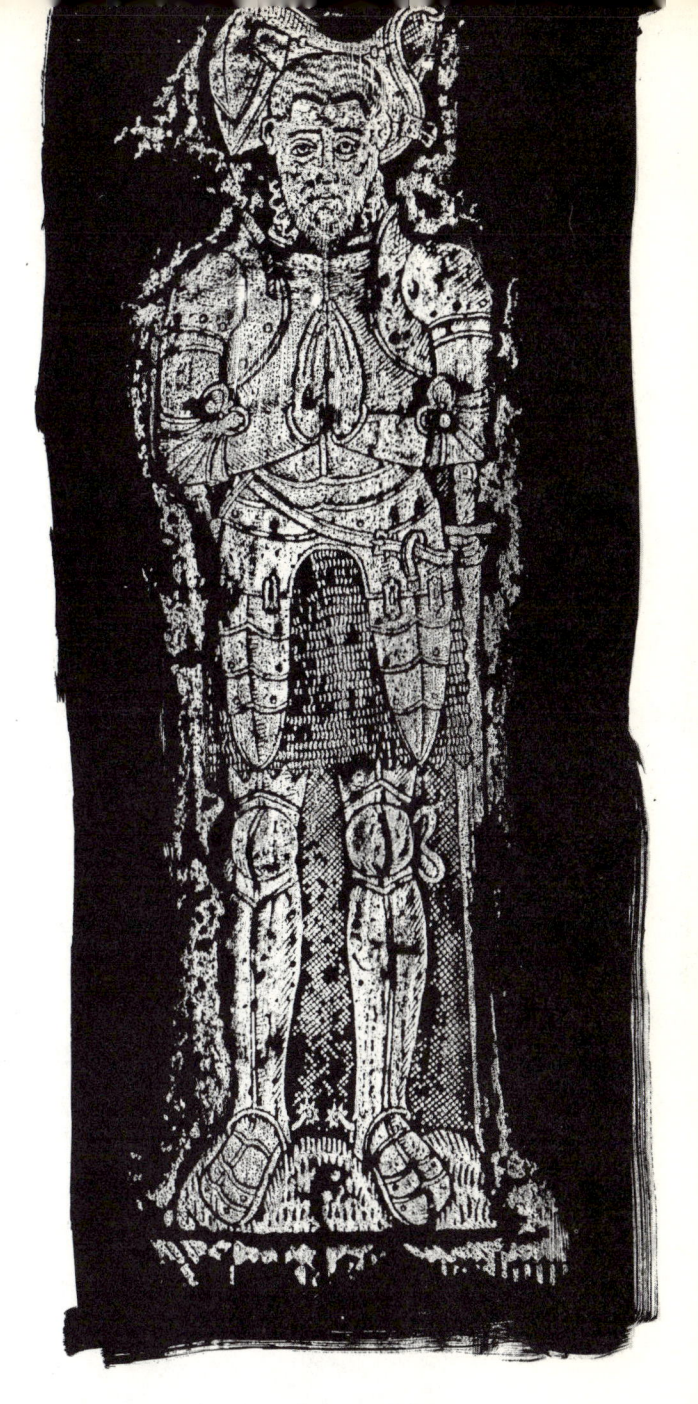

A reverse print can be made by rubbing with white candle-wax instead of heelball. The black is painted in later with ebony stain; the wax resists the stain, and the rubbing appears in white on a dark background. *Be careful with the stain, as it will be difficult to clean up if you make a mess.*

Potato and Cork Prints

Now you need the roller and glass again. This time you will be pressing the printing surface down onto the paper with your hand, not the paper onto the printing surface. The simplest things to print from in this way are potatoes, and corks, which have a ready-made textured surface.

Only water-based printing inks are suitable for printing with potatoes, as these mainly consist of watery fibres. Cut a large potato in half, and with a kitchen knife cut out a shape from the smooth surface. This will leave a raised pattern.

You must leave potatoes to dry out for an hour at least before printing with them.

First roll up a layer of ink on the glass; then press the printing surface into the ink and onto the paper.

Simple designs can easily be built up from the same shape.

Printing from Linoleum

You can make more varied designs by cutting into a block of lino. This can be bought at most art shops, or you may find a few spare pieces at home. Vinyl floor coverings are not suitable, unfortunately.

To start with you will need three basic tools: the V-shaped cutter, the U-shaped gouge and the cutting knife, which is used for cutting away large areas of lino. These normally come with separate handles, and you can buy them at art shops.

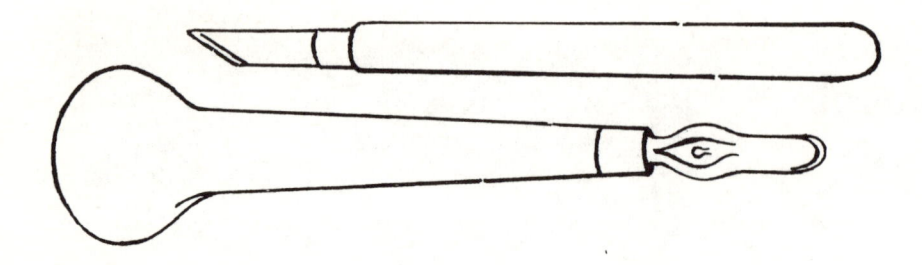

Before cutting the lino, warm it in front of a fire or a radiator, as you will find that it becomes much more supple and easier to use.

Experiment with lines and textures to get the feel of your tools and the lino. Always cut away from you. To cut curves and circles you will find it easier if you turn the lino slowly round with your other hand while you are cutting.

The areas you have cut will appear white when printed, and you should not cut right down to the string netting at the base of the lino, as this weakens it. A shallow cut is quite sufficient. When you have completed your design it is now ready for printing.

Roll up plenty of ink on the glass, and then roll up the lino, working the roller in all directions to make an even coat of ink. Then take a slightly damp piece of paper and place it over the block.

Smooth down the paper with your fingers, from the centre outwards, making sure that there are no cockles or air bumps underneath. Burnish the whole area with the back of a tablespoon to make sure the pressure is even.

Lift up one corner to see if the ink has taken, and carefully peel the paper off the block from one side. Pin down all four corners onto a piece of cardboard to prevent it from curling up as it dries.

You can make more variety with a coloured background. If you stick squares of coloured tissue paper onto a sheet of white paper before you print, you will have a multi-coloured background to your one-colour design. In this case the paper should not be damped.

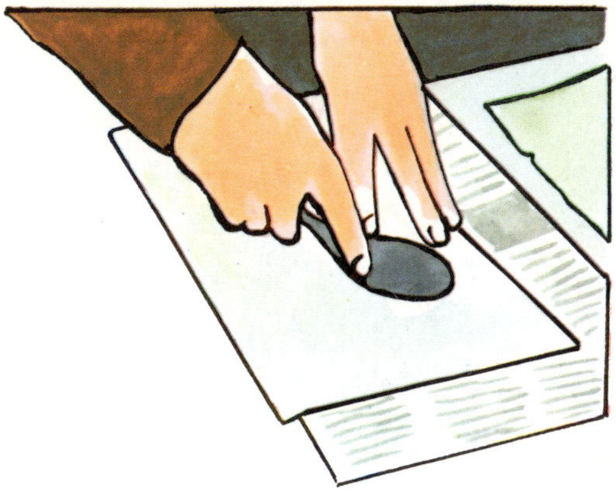

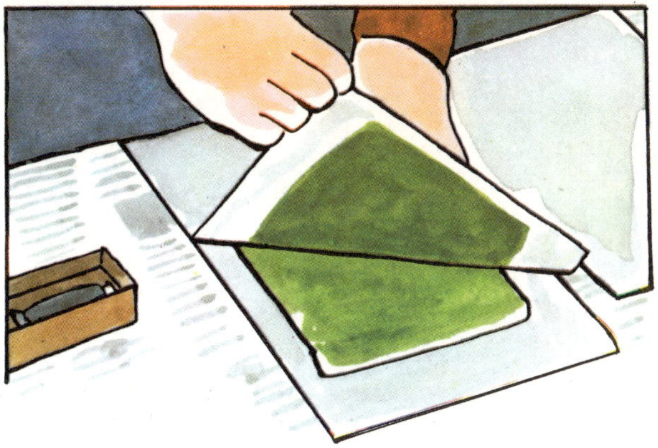

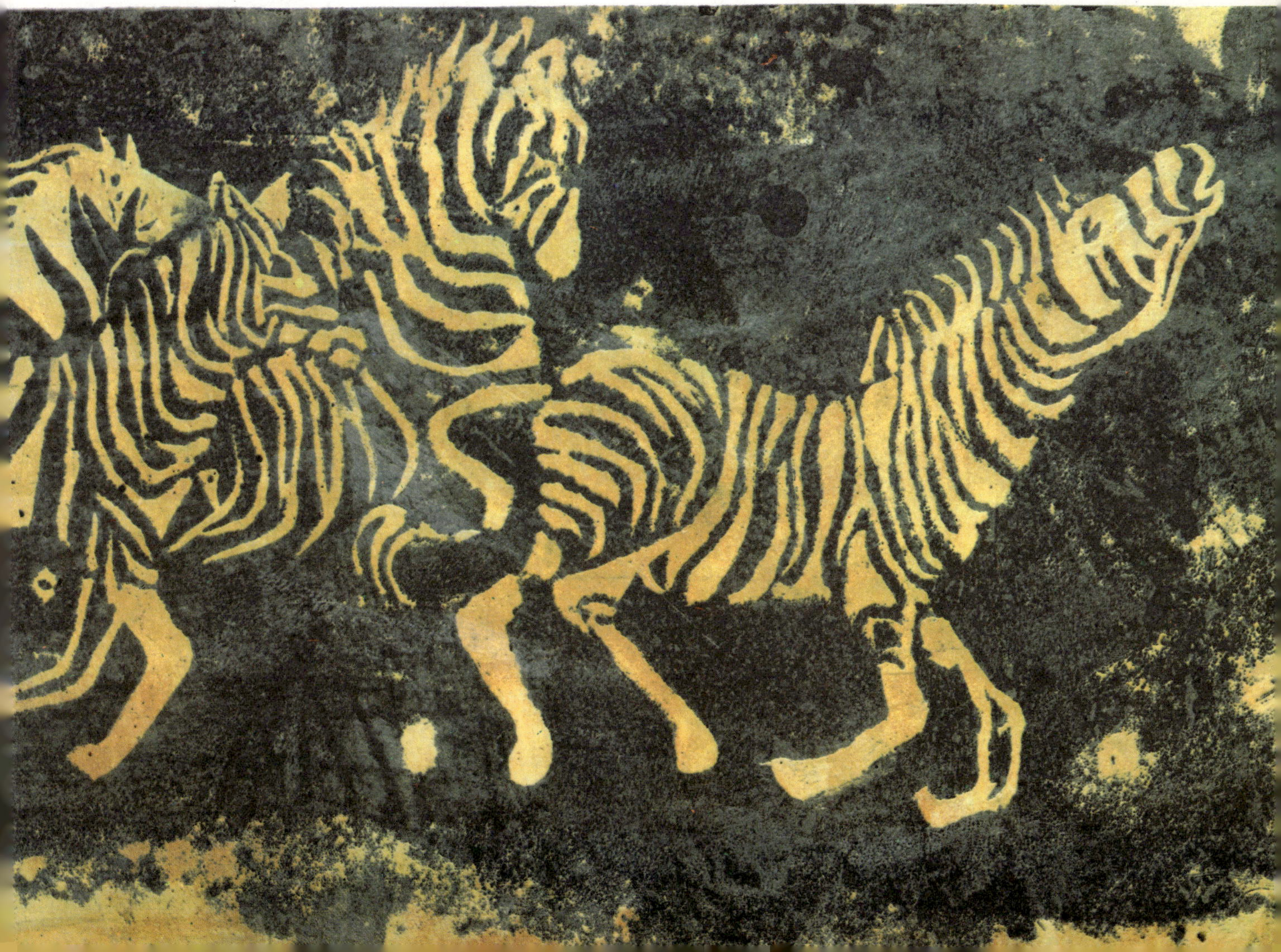

String and Felt Collage Blocks

Pieces of string or felt can be stuck onto blocks of wood or thick cardboard with contact glue. Leave these to dry firmly in place, and then roll them up and print as before (see page 14). The raised surfaces will print in the colour of the ink. Don't use too much pressure with the roller.

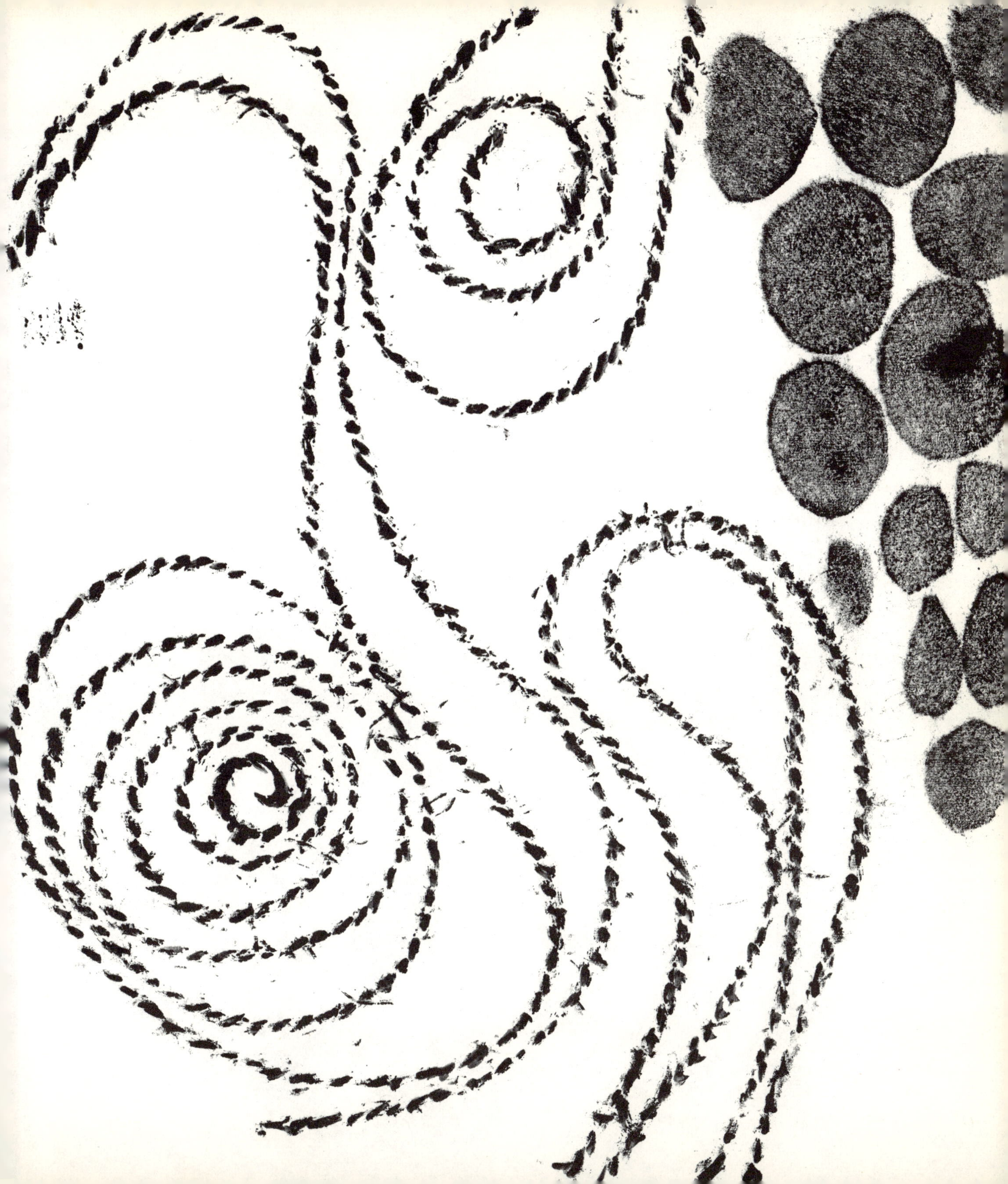

Don't be content just to copy the illustrations in this book. Try out other ways of printing from everyday things, and experiment with designs, textures and colour. You can make your own pictures, greeting cards, posters; you'll never run out of things to do.

Lino cut by A. Pendle